D0734275

MILLIONAIRE
by 40

MILLIONAIRE
by 40

100 Secrets
to Creating Wealth–
Not Taught In School

JEFF SAVAGE

Published by Buckeye Publishing
www.Millionairebyforty.com

10 9 8 7 6 5   4   3   2   1

PUBLISHER'S CATALOGING-IN-PUBLICATION DATA
Savage, Jeff.

Millionaire by 40: 100 secrets to creating wealth—not taught in
school / Jeff Savage. — Maumee, Ohio : Buckeye Publishing, 2005.
           p.   ; cm.
           ISBN 0-9743844-1-0
Library of Congress Control Number: 2004112960

1. Young adults—Finance, Personal. 2. Finance, Personal.
3. Financial security. 4. Motivation (Psychology) I. Title.

HG179 .S38   2005
332.024/0084/2—dc22   CIP

Printed in the United States of America

Text design by To The Point Solutions
www.tothepointsolutions.com

To my wife, Carol.
My soul mate and the love of my life.

Contents

Preface . . . 11

Acknowledgments . . . 13

Introduction . . . 17

100 SECRETS

1. Have Big Expectations 2. Your Attitude is Your Most Important Asset 3. The Cool Crowd Today Won't be Cool Later 4. Stay Away From Risky Behaviors 5. No Earrings or Tattoos 6. Take A Lot of Photos 7. Keep Your Car Well-Maintained 8. Don't Smoke 9. Talk in Front of Groups 10. Earn a College Degree 11. Attend College Away From Home 12. Attend a University in Your Home State 13. Take Accounting and Finance Classes 14. Have Fun in College—But Graduate on Time 15. Graduate From College Debt-Free 16. Once You Graduate From College It's Time to Work 17. After College, Playing Sports Should be a Low Priority 18. Live at Home After College 19. Buy Your Car, Don't Lease It 20. Don't Buy a Brand-New Car 21. Drive Your Car Until It Has 200,000+ Miles 22. Eat and Drink at Home 23. When You Move Out on Your Own, Find

a Roommate 24. Remain Single as Long as Possible 25. Get Out of Your Protective Shell 26. Choosing Your Career 27. Choose a Career With Great Earning Potential 28. Select Your Job Wisely and Stay There 29. Work Almost Every Waking Hour Building Your Career 30. Stay Focused on Your Career 31. Be Absolutely Sold on Your Employer 32. Dress Professionally 33. Work Hard When You are Young 34. Be Organized 35. Ask Questions 36. It's About Delayed Gratification 37. Find Mentors Throughout Your Life 38. Earn Everything Yourself 39. Be On Time For Meetings 40. Treat Everyone Well 41. Be Genuine 42. Fear Failure 43. Read, Especially Books Written by Successful People in Your Field 44. Keep Up With Current Events 45. Know What's Happening Around You 46. Press On, Regardless 47. Sharpen Your People Skills 48. Don't Feel Sorry for Yourself 49. Don't Promise More Than You Can Deliver 50. Complete What You Start 51. Purchase Life Insurance When You're Young 52. Stay in Shape 53. Realize That You Are Always on Stage 54. Maintain Perfect Credit 55. Be Willing to Sacrifice Some Relationships 56. Sunday Through Thursday Nights are Not for Partying 57. Continue to Improve at Your Career 58. Do Not Call in Sick 59. Don't Waste Time 60. Don't Expect Anyone to Create Opportunities for You 61. Network 62. Remember People's Names 63. Buy What You Need, Not

What You Want 64. Choose Your Spouse Wisely
65. Don't Accept Money From Your Parents
66. Don't Become a Good Golfer 67. Stay Away
From Activities That Drain Cash 68. Exercise
Caution Before Signing Your Name 69. Spend Cash
70. Large Savings is Not Dependent On Large
Income 71. Volunteer Your Time 72. Walk Fast
73. Nothing Replaces Face-to-Face Communication
74. Listen, Don't Talk 75. Buy What You Need and
Move Forward 76. Provide Exact Directions 77. Send
Handwritten Thank-You Notes 78. Be Competitive
79. Use Personal Days Sparingly 80. Eat Healthy
Foods and Take Vitamins 81. Don't Run Away From
Your Debts 82. Take Calculated Financial Risks
Along the Way 83. Pre-Pay Your Bills in January
84. Set Your Sights on Forty 85. Buy the Best
Quality Merchandise You Can Afford 86. Embrace
Change 87. Simplify Everything 88. Be Accessible
89. Go Above and Beyond the Call of Duty
90. Technology is a Double-Edged Sword 91. Buy
Supplemental Insurance When You Have a Family
92. Let's Talk About Retirement 93. Transform on
Income-Generating Sources 94. Don't Even Think
About Social Security 95. Generate a Personal Net
Worth Statement Every Six Months 96. Diversify
Your Portfolio 97. A Solid Strategy to Build Your Net
Worth 98. After You've Built a Great Net Worth,
Donate 99. You May Have to Reinvent Yourself
100. The Future Has Never Been Brighter

FOOD FOR THOUGHT

Happiness is a Journey,
Not a Destination . . . 122

Success . . . 124

A Story to Live By . . . 125

The Rest of Your Life Begins
Where You Are Now . . . 128

George Brett on "How to
Play the Game" . . . 129

Six Ways to Beat Procrastination . . . 130

A New Day . . . 132

Failures . . . But Not Quite . . . 133

If I Had My Life to Live Over . . . 134

Preface

M ost of the books on how to acquire wealth are written for adults and by "super humans," people who obtained their financial independence in ways that are out of reach for the average person—like you and me. I wrote this book to explain how you can become a *Millionaire by 40* and gain personal fulfillment.

All you need is the drive to succeed and the ability to set goals.

When I was in my teens I developed habits that allowed me to accumulate great wealth and financial freedom by the time I was forty. *Millionaire by 40: 100 Secrets to Creating Wealth—Not Taught in School* lists the ideas and philosophies I embraced in order to reach my goal—the "secrets" I didn't learn in school.

This book provides you with a path that leads to financial success. It gives you the tools you'll need to secure your financial future. Obtaining wealth takes time and requires great discipline and sacrifice—but watching your monetary worth increase is a lot of fun! There are many rewards as you climb ever closer to your goal.

Over the years, I've realized the ascent to financial freedom can continue indefinitely, i.e., you may never reach the summit because once you develop these habits they will stay with you for life and you will continue to soar!

Millionaire by 40 contains one hundred habits and philosophies I've lived by since I was a teenager, one-liners and inspirational phrases that have motivated me (you will find these quotes at the bottom of each "secret" page), and some "Food for Thought."

After you've read this book, keep it in a conspicuous place so you can reference it whenever you need motivation. If you adopt these habits now, while you are young, you will achieve financial independence and personal fulfillment.

Even though forty may seem like an eternity away; it isn't. Time does fly—especially after college. If you don't want to be forever tied to a job, where your only freedom is a few vacation weeks a year, start reading and applying these secrets today.

Acknowledgments

The success I have achieved is largely due to the high degree of understanding my wife, Carol, has shown regarding any project I've deemed necessary to accomplish. We have had a great relationship for fourteen years (married for eight). I can't wait to see what the future holds for us. Carol is extremely successful in any endeavor she takes on and is a role model for all young women to follow.

I am forever indebted to my parents, Kate and the late John Savage. I was lucky to have grown up in an environment with much wisdom and understanding (as their most challenging child I experienced a lot of their understanding). Mom and Dad did a miraculous job raising nine children. My siblings and I truly were given a unique advantage in life just by sitting around the dinner table every night.

I would not be where I am today without the mentors I have been blessed with throughout my life.

My dad, who was truly the most complete man I will ever meet. If someone told me that I was 25 percent of what he was, my life would be considered a success.

Thank you to Chris Anderson, who at a young age taught me the value of hard work and how to have fun at it.

Thank you to Dave Yeager, who taught me the value of being an entrepreneur and how to sell creatively.

And last but not least, thank you to Andy Malcolm, who gave me the opportunity to be his business partner. Saying yes to him turned out to be the best business decision of my life. I have yet to meet someone with such people skills and operational skills to navigate a very complex company. All that aside, Andy is a great friend and a pleasure to hang out with. We've solved many of the world's problems during our treasured conversations.

I could not have asked for a better group of siblings. I am proud of each of them and am amazed at the path in life that each has taken. We were raised to be independent, which obviously was taken to heart.

Carol's parents, "Big Lou" and JoAnn, and her four siblings have done a masterful job molding Carol into the person I was so fortunate to marry. They are a close group and value family more than any other family I have ever known.

I could write paragraphs about the great times I've had with my closest friends: Tom "Bubba" Irmen, Mike "Buckwheat" Ryan, Fritz "Fritzie" Rudolph, Don "Dynamic" Dougherty, Bob "Bobbie" Mollenkopf, and Ed "Big Ed" Steyer. I will keep the memories to myself, however, as this is a book written for young adults.

When it is all said and done, family and friends are what is most important in my life.

I will never be able to pay any of you back for all you have given me. Thank you for a great life.

There are two types of people in this world:

    A: Those who spend and save what's left.

    B: Those who save and spend what's left.

The people in Group A always work for the people in Group B.

John F. Savage

Introduction

Many of the secrets I reveal in this book can be—should be—embraced while you're still in high school or college. Saving money must always be a top priority, no matter how young or old you are. If nothing else, remember this: **You will never become financially independent if you do not master the skill of saving money.**

I will repeat this over and over because it is the most important secret.

To maximize the compounding effect of interest you must start saving all you can, as soon as you can. The cost of waiting is too expensive.

The chart on the following page shows in black and white how costly each year you delay saving money can be to your financial freedom.

If at age twenty you deposit $200 a week in a tax-deferred retirement plan that pays an average of eight percent interest, and you continue this habit until you reach age sixty-five, you can accumulate over four million dollars! If you wait until you are thirty, you will accumulate about two million dollars. And, if you don't start saving until you're forty, you will only have about $800,000.

This chart makes the cost of procrastination painfully clear. DON'T WAIT. Start now.

If you start saving $200 a week when you are

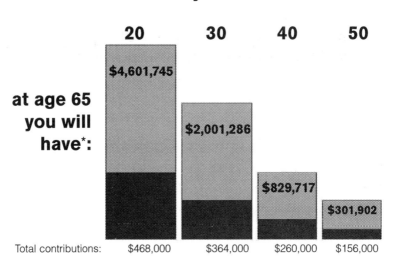

* This example is based on weekly contributions to a tax-deferred retirement plan that earns an annual rate of 8% compounded monthly.

100 SECRETS

1. Have Big Expectations

WHEN I was sixteen I had it all figured out. I was making $4.80 an hour loading fertilizer bags onto farm trucks. I knew if I could accumulate $300,000 I would be set for life. Little did I know how little I knew! When you are young, a great paying hourly job may seem like big money—but it isn't. You must become a professional, own a company, become a high- commissioned salesperson, or a business executive to reach a high-income level. Get yourself on a path now to fall into one of these categories. Step out of the box. There is absolutely no reason why you can't end up better off financially than the environment you grew up in. Set your sights high. Don't settle for mediocrity. I've often thought there was a fine line separating very successful people and those just making it. A few adjustments made at an early age could have pushed some underachievers into the realm of financial independence. You are only limited by what your mind tells you—so shoot high.

> *"I prefer the errors of enthusiasm to the indifference of wisdom."* -Anatole France

2. Your Attitude is Your Most Important Asset

Don't you hate associating or dealing with people who have bad attitudes? If your answer is yes, why would you ever want to carry around a negative attitude? A person with a great attitude will always out-perform a more skilled person with a poor attitude. You cannot allow any external factors to affect your attitude because a negative attitude will cripple your career. Remember: Your attitude, not your aptitude, will determine your altitude.

"Act like you expect to get into the end zone."
- Joe Paterno

3. The Cool Crowd Today Won't be Cool Later

When I think about the cool kids from my younger years, they were the troublemakers, wise guys, and partyers. There can be a great temptation to hang out with the cool group, but just be aware that they more than likely will not be successful at forty. These kids will be borrowing money and working for the kids that weren't so cool. You may think you are missing something by not hanging out with the in-crowd, but this group is normally insecure and actually has respect for the kids who take the middle road, even though they don't show it.

"The biggest myth in sports is that of the 'natural player.' Remember that Michael Jordan was cut from his high school team." - Bill Bradley

4. Stay Away From Risky Behaviors

There are many choices you can make when you are young that can have profound consequences on your life and can ruin your chances of financial success. If you drive drunk and either seriously injure or kill someone you will bury yourself so deep with all of the ramifications that it will take years to recover. If you have unprotected sex and a pregnancy results, the responsibilities of raising a child can force you out of school and derail you from the goals you had set. Inflicting permanent damage on your mind or body through the abuse of drugs or other risky behaviors or stunts can render you incapable of handling job responsibilities. Everything you do has consequences—both good and bad. Always remember that more often than not it is your strengths that will get you into trouble—not your weaknesses. Think about it!

"Reputation is what you are perceived to be. Character is what you are." - John Wooden

5. No Earrings or Tattoos

Picture yourself at age sixty with several tattoos and holes wherever holes are being pierced these days. I think you will agree, it is not a pretty picture. If your goal is to work an hourly job your entire life, then hang out in all of the tattoo and body piercing salons you want. If you permanently mark your body in places that can be seen, you will eliminate your chances of finding a first-class job because employers hire clean-cut, respectable looking employees that will represent their company in a professional manner. What you think is cool and trendy now could damage you for life.

> *"We tire of the pleasures we take, but never of those we give."* - Petit Senn

6. Take A Lot of Photos

One big regret I have is the lack of photos to chronicle my younger life. I wasn't big on taking pictures so most of my childhood is strictly faded memories. I didn't start using a camera until I was an adult, which I regret. Now that I am older, I wish I had carried a camera around with me to capture a lot of the moments I experienced. There are many events I have forgotten that I could have kept alive if I had only snapped some pictures. (This is an unusual chapter to appear in a financial book but this is important. Acquire a camera soon—and start taking pictures!)

"There is no greater reward than to make a fundamental difference in someone's life."
- Sister Mary Rose McGeady (children's advocate)

7. Keep Your Car Well-Maintained

You may be asking yourself, What does car maintenance and cleanliness have to do with financial freedom? A car is usually your first major financial responsibility in life, so it is a good time to start developing positive habits. Caring for your car requires organizational skills, and keeping things clean is a habit you must possess. No one wants to be associated with a slob. Automobile manufacturers make cars that require little maintenance and, if you follow the maintenance schedule, the car will last longer and cost you a lot less to own. Write up a maintenance schedule and stick to it.

> *"The reward of a thing well done is to have done it."*
> - Ralph Waldo Emerson

8. Don't Smoke

Not only is smoking detrimental to your physical health, it is terrible for your financial health. At the time of this printing, cigarettes cost about $4.00 a pack. The impact of not being able to save this money can be quite significant, especially if you have a pack-a-day habit. Some people do not like to be associated with smokers and, in business, this can cost you a lot of money. Some view smoking as a weakness and don't want to deal with weak people. Others can't stand the odor and general unsanitary conditions that surround some smokers. Also think of the time a smoker wastes. Smoking is a very time-consuming habit. If that time was spent working, how much more money could that smoker have accumulated over his/her lifetime? And speaking of lifetime, a smoker's is not usually a long one.

> *"Success is simply a matter of luck. Ask any failure."*
> - Earl Wilson

9. Talk in Front of Groups

It is never too early to hone your public speaking skills. Take all of the communication and public speaking classes you can because if you plan on rising to the top in any career it will require making presentations in front of groups of people. When I listen to speakers I take notes on the techniques they utilize, along with good lines I feel I can use down the road. Some humor is key to being a good speaker because usually your subject matter will put even the most interested audience to sleep. Always remember: A short talk is greatly appreciated.

> *"Behold the turtle. He makes progress only when he sticks his neck out."* - James Conant

10. Earn a College Degree

It is a rare person who excels financially and does not have a college degree. A college degree can help you get a job opportunity that you won't get if you don't have a degree. College teaches many things, like time management, how to interact with other people, how to prepare, how to live independently, how to think logically, etc. Remember, though, that no one owes you anything just because you have a degree. How you perform will determine your success. If you are lazy and have a bad attitude, your degree will mean little.

> *"In this life, the big, strong guys are always taking from the smaller, weaker guys but . . . the smart take from the strong."* - Unknown

11. Attend College Away From Home

This is one of the few times I will suggest you spend more money than you have to. Living at home while attending college is definitely less expensive than going away, but the experiences and memories of attending college away from home are priceless. This is the best time of your life and you need to learn to be independent. You will make lifelong friends that you would not if you stayed at home. When you remove yourself from your hometown you learn how to interact with strangers, how to make smart decisions, and how to survive in stressful situations—on your own. You may spend an extra $30,000 in living expenses over four years but it is a small price to pay for life-changing experiences.

> "I believe half the unhappiness in life comes from people being afraid to go straight at things."
> - Unknown

12. Attend a University in Your Home State

This is purely a financial decision. There are great universities in other states, which include some of the big-name colleges, but they can cost eight times the amount of your in-state university. The problem with going to an out-of-state university is that you pay so much more because you don't live in the state, even though you end up with the same degree as the in-state students. If you are determined to attend an out-of-state school, hopefully it is for a degree you can't get anywhere else and it lands you a premium job to pay down the mountain of debt you will have accumulated.

> *"I don't try to jump over seven-foot bars. I look around for one-foot bars that I can step over.*
> - Warren Buffet

13. Take Accounting and Finance Classes

This is the biggest regret I have about my college years. I took a few entry-level accounting and finance classes but only studied just enough to get through them. I did not take these classes as seriously as I did my other classes because I knew I was going to be in sales and thought I did not need to know "that stuff." I pay for this mistake daily when I hire others for advice that I should be able to figure out myself. The fact is you will likely need to understand and be able to evaluate financial statements. Plus, you are more valuable and more marketable to employers if you have a strong financial background.

> "I never did anything worthwhile by accident, nor did any of my inventions come by accident; they came by work. - Thomas Edison

14. Have Fun in College—
But Graduate On Time

College is definitely the greatest time of your life, but limit it to a four-year party. If you need to catch up, attend classes in the summer—but get out on time and get to work. The sooner you graduate and start banking some money, the faster you will reach financial independence. Some people I know made college a career and they started accumulating money way too late. Now they regret not putting their noses to the grindstone and graduating in four years. Other people will get their undergraduate degree, and then spend more years getting a master's degree. If you truly need a master's degree to get to where you want to go, by all means get one. But don't obtain a master's degree to delay your entry into the working world.

> *"The haves and have-nots can often be traced back to the dids and did-nots."* - D.O. Flynn

15. Graduate From College Debt-Free

You may think this is impossible, but if you attend a state university in your home state and you are getting a basic, undergraduate degree, it can be done. Start saving your money in high school and continue to work in college. I worked two jobs in college, operated my own business, had an absolutely wonderful time, and still graduated in four years debt-free. In college I operated a business that sold printed glasses, T-shirts, etc. to organizations on campus, including fraternities and sororities. I am not saying to do this, but an enterprising mind can find great opportunities to make money. Most of the people I associated with did not work in college and they graduated with a pile of debt. Again, this delayed the point when they could start saving money, which you already know is financially disastrous.

> "The three great essentials to achieve anything worthwhile are first, hard work; second, stick-to-itiveness; and third, common sense." - Unknown

16. Once You Graduate From College It's Time to Work

Some people travel for a year or so after graduation so they can "see the world." This only puts them further in debt and delays when they start to save money. There is plenty of time to see the world after you've made it—GET TO WORK! Once you graduate, the party is over! Don't move to a big party city after graduation so you can work and party four nights a week. Instead visit these cities on weekends a few times a year, have fun, and get back home where your expenses are under control. Big cities are expensive to live in, and all of your take-home pay can be spent just trying to survive. The first few years after college are critical because this is when you can put away a large percentage of your take-home pay. If you must move to a big city, find an inexpensive place to live. It might not be in the most desirable location, but you must put a large portion of your take-home pay into savings.

> *"I think we should follow a simple rule: If we can take the worst, take the risk."* - Dr. Joyce Brothers

17. After College, Playing Sports Should be a Low Priority

I am not against participating in organized athletics, but you must realize that after college, your chance of making a living in athletics has passed and your career must now be your #1 priority. Some of my friends would never be late, or heaven forbid, miss a softball game, even if it meant missing out on a career enhancing opportunity. These guys had their priorities messed up and are still struggling to pay bills and get ahead in life. There are leagues that you can participate in that have their games on weekends and those are the leagues to get involved with. When you realize how much easier you can get injured as you get older, you will eventually eliminate organized sports altogether and focus on other ways to stay in shape.

> *"We are what we repeatedly do."* - Unknown

18. Live at Home After College

Living with Mom and Dad may not be the preferred housing arrangement after you graduate from college—but the money you can bank by not paying for rent, utilities, and food will add up in a big way. This is when you can really put money away because you have your first real job without a lot of personal expenses. You can build a financial base and hone your saving habits. There does come a time, however, when you must leave the nest and make it on your own; but if you can stand to live at home for a few years, the savings will make a dramatic impact on your net worth down the road.

"It's a sobering thought: When Mozart was my age, he had been dead for two years." - Tom Lehrer

19. Buy Your Car, Don't Lease It

Automobile dealerships make more money leasing cars than selling cars. They try to lure you in with a low lease payment, but in the fine print, you will read about the large down payment needed, the short term of the lease, and low mileage restraints. If leasing is best for the dealership, it is not best for you.

"Don't learn the tricks of the trade—learn the trade."
- John Charlton

20. Don't Buy a Brand-New Car

By purchasing a used car with low mileage, you can save up to 30 percent off the price of a brand-new car. Make sure you are not buying an ex-rental car, as they traditionally get beat up pretty bad. Instead buy an off-lease or manufacturer's executive car. The first car you purchase should be a mid-sized car, then you can move up as you get older and are financially secure. Your buddies will buy the cool, high-dollar cars and then be forced to buy the mid-sized ones as they get older because they did not sacrifice when they were young. I prefer to buy cars with less than 30,000 miles on them and, before I take possession, I have the dealer change all of the fluids and filters so I am starting fresh with my maintenance program.

"Ignore the fans, the fans can't play." - Unknown

21. Drive Your Car Until It Has 200,000+ Miles

Your car, especially when you are young, is strictly for transportation. It is an expense not a fashion statement. Changing cars every couple of years because you want the newest model or you are bored with the same old car is a major mistake. This habit will cost you dearly as you try to get ahead. Cars are now built to last 250,000 miles as long as you do the required maintenance.

> *"Time is infinitely more precious than money and there is nothing common between them. You cannot accumulate time; you cannot borrow time; you can never tell how much you have left in the Bank of Life. Time is life."* - Israel Davidson

22. Eat And Drink at Home

Eating at restaurants and drinking at bars when you are young will significantly affect the amount of money you can save. You can eat at home for 30 percent of what it costs to eat at a restaurant and if you have a couple of drinks at home before you hit the bars (with your designated driver of course) you will save another 70 percent. Save restaurants for special occasions while you are building your net worth. Fifty dollars here and fifty dollars there can add up to hundreds of thousands of dollars over time.

"You can't fall out of a hole." - Unknown

23. When You Move Out on Your Own, Find a Roommate

S plitting living expenses in half will allow you to bank significantly more than if you live by yourself. Living with a roommate is something you will be glad you did when you are older. I had a roommate until I was thirty. We lived in the least expensive part of town (within reason) and controlled our expenses so we could save as much as possible. You can probably save an extra $6,000 a year by having a roommate; which, when compounded, will add up to hundreds of thousands of dollars (if you do this for several years) by the time you retire.

> *"Don't be humble. You're not that great."*
> - Golda Meir

24. Remain Single as Long as Possible

Staying single until you're in your thirties has many benefits. You change a lot between the ages of twenty and thirty; and the spouse you want at twenty is not the same one you'll want when you're thirty. Plus, it is much easier to save money when you are single because you can live with a roommate for much less than a mortgage. When you get married, you may be supporting another person and/or upgrading your lifestyle (you may not be able to convince your spouse to live in a $300 a month basement apartment in the hood). Also, the longer you wait to start a family has a dramatic impact on your financial future. If you start too early you can get yourself in such a deep hole that you may never surface.

> *"Nothing in the world can take the place of persistence. Talent will not; nothing is more common than unsuccessful men with talent. Genius will not; unrewarded genius is almost a proverb. Education will not; the world is full of educated derelicts. Persistence and determination are omnipotent."*
> - Calvin Coolidge

25. Get Out of Your Protective Shell

When I was in my late teens and early twenties I liked to test myself by going into the inner city to play basketball. I thought it made me a tougher person and taught me how to handle myself in all sorts of situations. I quickly realized that not everyone in the world is nice and that some people want to hurt and steal from others. If you are only exposed to nice, friendly people while you are growing up, the real world will hit you like a ton of bricks. Go out of your way to meet and interact with all sorts of different people. Get out of your comfort zone and go mix it up a bit. These experiences will do a lot to make you street smart, which wins out over book smart.

"Never confuse movement with action."
- Ernest Hemingway

26. Choosing Your Career

Many people say they want to work at a job they love. I've never loved my job per se, but I have always worked in a field that I was good at and enabled me to build a great net worth. Don't get me wrong, I've liked the jobs I've had, but they have all been hard work. I would have loved other careers, but I would not have reached my financial goals. I will work at a job I love when I don't need the income. Having said that, if you want to work at a job you love and you are satisfied with the income (you may be fortunate that this job provides a large salary), then go for it—but don't have any regrets.

> *"Progress means taking risks, for you can't steal home and keep your foot on third base."* - Unknown

27. Choose a Career With Great Earning Potential

There are thousands of dead-end jobs out there—DO NOT APPLY! Select a career where there is potential to make a lot of money if you perform well. Make sure there is no ceiling as to what you can earn. A salaried or hourly job will be your guarantee that you will never get rich. If you plan on working very hard, make it worth your while.

"*Everywhere is walking distance if you have the time.*" - Steven Wright

28. Select Your Job Wisely and Stay There

People who move from job to job to job are not usually very successful. You must select a career that has great potential, understand that you probably will not be an overnight success, and then work very hard to hit your goals. It sometimes takes five years of hard work before you reap the rewards, but you must accept this going in and not get impatient and jump to another job. The grass is normally not greener on the other side, and if you switch, you'll have to start from scratch building another career. Honest effort is always rewarded. As long as your initial job selection is good, persevere and make it happen. There are thousands of dead-end jobs—do not apply! If a truly great opportunity comes along, study it closely so you don't take any steps backward and take the opportunity if your gut tells you that it is in your best interest.

"Faded ink is better than the clearest mind."
- Unknown

29. Work Almost Every Waking Hour Building Your Career

If you sacrifice your nights and part of your weekend building your career, you can't help but be successful. I know many less qualified people who, through sheer hard work, enjoy greater success than their more qualified counterparts. I can't stress this enough—you must make sure you are spending your time doing the right things that will increase your income. Some people work long hours but they either procrastinate or focus on things that don't advance their careers. The bank doesn't care how many hours you've worked, just the amount of the deposit slip in your hand.

> "If you're not practicing, just remember—someone, somewhere, is practicing. And when you two meet, given roughly equal ability, he will win. Do not lose simply because you didn't make the effort."
> - Bill Bradley

30. Stay Focused on Your Career

As you are building your career, you might be tempted to create a second source of income in what is referred to as a "side job." The problem with a side job is that it diverts your effort and focus away from your full-time job. Any extra money you earn at the side job will probably be proportionately lost at your full-time job. Most of us are not talented enough to navigate two careers successfully at the same time. More than likely you will fail at one or both jobs. Once you've found a rewarding career, give it your all and don't deviate. Your full-time employer will eventually realize he/she is not getting your undivided attention and effort at work and may make your side job the only job you have.

> *"Minutes are worth more than money. Spend them wisely."* - Thomas Murphy

31. Be Absolutely Sold on Your Employer

If you are not totally sold on the company you work for and the products it represents, it will reflect in your performance. You must have a passion for what you do because that enthusiasm is what makes you successful. If you think your competitor is better than your employer, then they will win the majority of the time. If you're not on the right team, get off of it and join the team you feel is the best. It is possible that several companies in the same industry honestly believe they have the best service and products. If this is the case, the people that work the hardest to service their clientele and convince them that they are the company to do business with will win in the marketplace.

> *"A lot of people run a race to see who's the fastest. I run to see who has the most guts."* - Steve Prefontaine

32. Dress Professionally

It is wise to spend money on quality dress clothes and shoes. You need to portray a successful, professional image because people want to associate with successful people. You will have an edge on someone who dresses casually or who portrays a sloppy image. Even in a so-called casual industry, you want to stand out to let your customers know you are serious about your business and you are the best person for them to work with. Your clothing is an investment in your future. I purchase all of my dress clothes at Nordstrom. I wait for the two big annual sales they have and then I buy great clothes at a discounted price from knowledgeable sales consultants.

"The buck stops here." - Harry S. Truman

33. Work Hard When You are Young

Your energy level is higher and you have fewer responsibilities at twenty-one than you will have at forty. Use these early years to work 12-hour days to build your career. This will take some sacrifice—but you will be glad you did it when you are older and you have a well-established career. Yes, working hard now may affect your "quality of life," but few people excel at their careers if they don't take the time to build them. Get to work now. You will have a better quality of life as you advance in your career. Your friends who did not put their nose to the grindstone will struggle their whole lives just to keep ahead of the bills.

"No mistakes, no experience; no experience, no wisdom." - Stanley Goldstein

34. Be Organized

You should develop good organizational skills at a young age. Clutter in your life impedes you from making clear, calculated decisions that can affect how you end up long term. It is impossible to be disorganized and also be successful. Every facet of your life must be in order, not just your business. You will have several things going on at once, and if you are not well organized your accomplishments will be limited. You need to know where you are at all times, both personally and professionally, so things don't fall through the cracks or get misplaced.

"When your work speaks for itself, don't interrupt."
- Henry Kaiser

35. Ask Questions

In an attempt to look smart, many people will not ask questions, which in reality, keeps them stupid forever. When you ask questions of someone you make that person feel important. They get a chance to show you how smart they are. If, however, you try to fake your way through a situation because your ego won't allow you to ask for more information and you make a mistake, you will lose your credibility and possibly your trust with the person with whom you are dealing. Once a person can't rely on or trust you, your relationship with them is jeopardized. I want to know everything about issues I am dealing with and am not embarrassed one bit to say three of the most important words in the English language: I DON'T KNOW!

"Luck is a matter of preparation meeting opportunity." - Oprah Winfrey

36. It's About Delayed Gratification

The things you think you need in your twenties are not what you would buy in your thirties. Therefore, when you start to make purchases on your own only spend money on what you need to survive and bank all of the rest. Wait until you are financially secure, hopefully in your late thirties or early forties, before you start buying the luxuries life has to offer, i.e., when you're twenty-five it is impossible to collect valuable cars and save money at the same time. If you do not exercise a high degree of self-discipline, you will never become financially independent. The earlier in life that you are willing to sacrifice will determine how quickly you become financially independent. You have to wait until you have "made it" before you start throwing your money at expensive hobbies. It is hard to wait, but you'll be glad you did.

"Skate to where the puck is going, not where it has been." - Wayne Gretsky

37. Find Mentors Throughout Your Life

A mentor is a person you look up to with great respect and try to emulate. I have had the honor of having four mentors at various times in my life. I closely watched everything they did and molded my personality after theirs. These people took me under their wing because they knew I was serious about learning from them and I was willing to work as hard and as long as it took to gain their respect. It is easy to identify mentors, but they will not teach you if you are undeserving of their time. You must be 110 percent committed to your job before a mentor is going to spend precious time helping you. They need to see a little bit of them in you before they investment their time in you.

> "Enthusiasm is the greatest asset in the world. It beats money, power, and influence." - Henry Chester

38. Earn Everything Yourself

You won't ever feel a true sense of achievement in your career if you don't do it on your own. I've always liked being compensated for what I brought to the table. People who either inherit a company or join a family business, and get compensated well for little work, must have unfulfilling lives. On the other hand, I have seen people get into family businesses that were failing, revolutionize them and make them successful, which must bring a feeling of great accomplishment. To feel good about yourself and to gain the respect of your peers, control your destiny with your hard work and moxie. Don't get me wrong, at some point we all drink out of wells we didn't dig, but you need an opportunity to prove what you can do with your own talents.

"I was tied with the leaders in the race until the gun went off." - Unknown

39. Be On Time For Meetings

I am early for everything in my professional life. I want to show respect for everyone I work with, and being late for a meeting is disrespectful. If you arrive late, customers will assume that you are disorganized and undisciplined. Don't accumulate any black marks on your customers' or boss's score-card—and believe me, they keep score. I realize that some circumstances are out of your control and if they cause you to be late, make a courtesy call to the person you are supposed to meet.

"Life is not a dress rehearsal." - Rose Tremain

40. Treat Everyone Well

Everyone deserves to be treated politely and respectfully. Keep your ego in check because in the scheme of life you are not that important. People spend 98 percent of their time thinking about themselves, so if you ever thought people were thinking about how great you are, you were dead wrong. Remember there are lots of people who are smarter and richer than you are, so remain levelheaded. Make all of the people you interact with feel important. Talk about them, not you, because they are more interested in themselves anyway. You will have more friends if you are interested in the other person instead of trying to make them become interested in you. The person you treat badly could become someone you need something from on your road to success, or they could become a superior at work who will pay you back by stalling your career or eliminating you altogether.

> *"Be kind, for everyone you meet is fighting a hard battle."* - Plato

41. Be Genuine

People who go overboard being nice and it is evident that this is not their regular personality are irritating. You see a lot of this in social and business settings. People who behave like this stick out like a sore thumb and they make those with whom they associate with feel apprehensive. People like genuine people. Don't worry if you aren't flamboyant, most successful people are just good, solid citizens, who are what they are. They make everyone around them feel comfortable. The loudmouth or life of the party is usually an insecure person who is dying for attention.

If you think for a moment that you can fake enough people to get where you want to be in life, you're dead wrong. BE YOURSELF!

"Whatever you can do, or dream you can do, begin it. Boldness has genius, power, and magic in it. Begin it now." - Goethe

42. Fear Failure

A fear of failure may be my biggest motivation in attacking the world every day. I don't want to be looked upon as a failure or become a burden on anyone. For whatever reason, I am deathly afraid to fail. If you are, too, you'll do okay. You need a motivating factor to get you out of bed every morning. If you don't have one yet, picture yourself living on the streets to see if that helps.

> *"He who deliberates fully before taking a step will spend his entire life on one leg."* - Chinese proverb

43. Read, Especially Books Written by Successful People in Your Field

Become a sponge for wisdom and knowledge by reading as many books as you can. Books contain motivation and inspiration. No matter what occupation you've chosen, if you want to be successful, read books written by people who have achieved in your field. I have always been in sales and have probably read fifty books written by the top salespeople in the country. Some books were better than others, but I could always pull at least one or two great ideas from each book. Every idea molds you into being better at what you do, as long as you put the idea into action. Reading is a great habit to get into.

"The only time you find success before work is in the dictionary." - May V. Smith

44. Keep Up With Current Events

I can't believe the people I meet who are totally oblivious to what's happening in the world their living in. Subscribing to a daily newspaper is a must. Even if you only scan the headlines and read the stories that are of interest to you, you will know what is going on, in town and all over the globe. It is also a good idea to watch CNN and a financial news station, like CNBC, so you have a handle on the most recent news along with the health of the economy. You interact with people all day and you don't want to come across as being out of touch with current events.

> *"Formal education will earn you a living. Self-education will earn you a fortune. You determine how much of a fortune you will earn by how much self-education you decide to get."* - Jim Rohn

45. Know What's Happening Around You

The more perceptive you are, the better off you will do financially. The reason I say this is because getting ahead requires being able to read people and to react to what's happening around you. Some people have no clue what is going on; they live with what is dealt them. On the other hand, perceptive people are out in front, they anticipate what is going to happen; they are constantly processing details and getting ahead with every move they make. It's almost as though they have a sixth sense. Even if you don't have this sixth sense, you can become more observant.

> *"Don't think there are no crocodiles because the water is calm."* - Unknown

46. Press On, Regardless

Inevitably you will encounter several disappointments and defeats in your career and personal life. It is up to you to not let these times devastate you and stop your forward progress. Tough times never last forever. You must work through them, even if they seem like insurmountable circumstances. Losing isn't fatal, so press on. Better times are around the corner as long as you keep doing the right things. Honest effort is always rewarded.

"Fall seven times, stand up eight." - Unknown

47. Sharpen Your People Skills

There are some basic skills you should have when interacting with people. You should greet others with enthusiasm and a sincere smile. Lean forward and look the person in the eye to let them know you are focused on them. An occasional, appropriate, light touch is a great relationship builder. Discuss topics that they are interested in and nod with interest as they talk and you listen. Never try to get the other person interested and impressed with you—because it's not going to happen. As simple as these skills are, they are missing in the majority of conversations that I witness.

> *"You can make more friends in a month by being interested in them than in ten years by trying to get them interested in you."* - Charles L. Allen (*Roads to Radiant Living*)

48. Don't Feel Sorry for Yourself

Many people walk around like the world owes them something. If you think people are going to feel sorry for you, you're wrong! People spend 98 percent of their time thinking about themselves, which leaves very little time for them to feel sorry for you. Feeling sorry for yourself is wasted energy. Snap out of it! Get to work!

"If your ship doesn't come in, swim out to it."
- Jonathan Winters

49. Don't Promise More Than You Can Deliver

You never want to destroy your credibility because it is almost impossible to regain it. You want people to be able to depend on you. Be careful what you tell someone. Write down what you have promised to do. Your word must be gospel, no matter how difficult or expensive it is to keep. Make a handwritten note to yourself every time you tell someone you will do something and keep the note in front of you until you have completed the task. It is better to look someone in the eye and tell them you can't do something instead of telling them what they want to hear, and then not deliver. Be honest with people.

> *"When I was a young man, I observed that nine out of ten things I did were failures. I didn't want to be a failure, so I did ten times more work."*
> - George Bernard Shaw

50. Complete What You Start

My dad always told me that if I started something, carried it through, and completed it I would be in the top one percent of the country. I took his advice to heart because I wanted to be in the top one percent. This sounds like such a simple philosophy but it is rarely practiced. Make sure that whatever you start gets finished, no matter how long it takes or how much it costs. You will love the feeling of accomplishment when a project is completed. If you write down what you have committed to, you are more likely to complete it because you will not cross it off your list until it is finished. It is up to you if you want to be in the top one percent.

> *"Great runners never drop out of a race, even in the worst of circumstances. Once you do, you've given yourself an option for the future."* - Unknown

51. Purchase Life Insurance When You're Young

Buying universal life insurance when you are twenty-one is a lot less expensive than buying it at forty, when a lot of people wake up and realize they need it. I would suggest buying a $400,000 policy at age twenty-one and another $400,000 policy at age twenty-five. By the time I'm in my early forties the cash values in my life insurance polices will be built up to a point where I will not have to pay premiums. My policies are inflation adjusted; your situation may be different. Visit with an insurance person that you trust. You should look at insurance as a supplemental income for your family, so their quality of life does not change if something happens to you.

"He who laughs, lasts." - Mary Poole

52. Stay in Shape

Make sure to include a workout in your daily routine and stick with it for life. I suggest working out first thing in the morning because it is too easy to make excuses after a long day. People like to deal with people who are in shape and you will have much more energy and a better self-image if you are physically fit. On top of all that, you will get sick less often and live longer. I don't particularly like waking up before everyone else in the world to work out but I feel good about myself and have an edge on 98 percent of my competitors who quit exercising after high school.

> *"Most folks are about as happy as they make up their minds to be."* - Abraham Lincoln

53. Realize That You Are Always on Stage

No matter where you are, pretend someone you need to set a good example for is watching you. You will find that oftentimes you are being watched—and you don't know it. Think of all the times in your life when you've run into people you knew in a place you wouldn't have dreamed of. Were you thankful you weren't doing something that may have embarrassed you? I know of people who have been fired from their jobs because they were doing something stupid when they were on stage, and didn't realize they were being watched.

"Perception is reality." - Unknown

54. Maintain Perfect Credit

Pay every single bill you have before it is due. Your credit report must remain spotless because you will need bank support in life and banks do not loan money to people who don't pay their bills on time. If your credit is not perfect, you will be forced to borrow from secondary lenders, which means you will pay a higher interest rate. Don't buy anything you can't afford to pay back on time because nothing is worth ruining your credit.

"The Horse and Mule Association tried to outlaw the use of trucks and cars in the 1920s." - Unknown

55. Be Willing to Sacrifice Some Relationships

To be financially successful you will need to work long hours, so some things will have to give. Unfortunately, sometimes it will be relationships with certain people. Your close friends will always remain close, and those relationships must be held dear for life. You will, however, have to give up nights out with "the guys" and/or "the girls" in order to reach your financial goals. I do believe you can re-establish these relationships later.

> "Two roads diverged in a wood, and I took the one less traveled by. And that has made all the difference." - Robert Frost

56. Sunday Through Thursday Nights are Not for Partying

It is impossible to perform at peak efficiency if you were partying the night before a workday. You must utilize these nights preparing yourself for the next business day. Co-workers and customers can see it in your eyes if you went out the night before and, subconsciously, it puts doubts in their minds that you do not take your job very seriously. This is one of many judgment calls you will have to make. In the long term, you will be glad you stayed in. Don't worry; you're not missing much. The same people will be out on Friday and Saturday night.

"The question isn't at what age I want to retire, it's at what income." - George Foreman

57. Continue to Improve at Your Career

Don't get complacent in your career. Not only do you run the risk of losing your job, but also your income is probably going to become stagnant or decrease. As hard as it might be, you need to keep your pump primed so your career and income continue to grow. Find new and exciting ways to do your job. It will keep your passion and drive alive. Constantly challenge yourself so you get better at what you do.

> *"We judge ourselves by what we feel we are capable of doing, while others judge us by what we have already done."* - Henry Wadsworth Longfellow

58. Do Not Call in Sick

Just because employers typically provide five sick days to their employees doesn't mean they want you to use them or that you should use them. Employers know who abuses this policy and when it comes time to cut staff, these slackers are the first to go. If you eat healthy, take vitamins, and exercise regularly, you can dramatically reduce your chances of getting sick. I recently heard a woman talking about a new job she was interviewing for. She hoped the potential employer would not investigate her attendance background because she had taken advantage of every sick and personal day that was available. Let me tell you, most employers do check out attendance records. Just to let you know, she did not get the dream job she was hoping for. I wonder why.

> *"Make something happen before lunch."*
> - Irving (Swifty) Lazar

59. Don't Waste Time

We are only on this earth for a short period. Hopefully you have a lot you need to accomplish. I always have a list of projects and can't wait until I have the time to get to them. The statistics on how much time people spend watching television or playing on the Internet is sickening. Busy, efficient people are the ones in the most demand because they make things happen. Procrastination drives me crazy. There is no excuse for it. Address what you need to accomplish and get it done—now!

> "Every time you wake up and ask yourself, 'What good things am I going to do today?' remember that when the sun goes down at sunset, it will take a part of your life with it." - India proverb

60. Don't Expect Anyone to Create Opportunities for You

Some people expect their employers to take care of them and provide them opportunities for success. Let me help you—YOU'RE ON YOUR OWN! You must make it happen every day you go to work and develop your own opportunities because you control your destiny. Someone recently said to me, "To be as successful as you are, you must have been at the right place at the right time." I felt like punching this guy. Successful people work hard and being at the right place at the right time is a by-product of the hard work. Take a position in a company that you feel has great potential—and then the rest is up to you. Doing it yourself is far more rewarding than having something given to you. You will have more self-esteem and a true sense of accomplishment that you did it on your own.

"If opportunity doesn't knock, build a door."
- Unknown

61. Network

Meet as many people as you can and let them know what you do. Business cards are inexpensive, so hand out hundreds of them. Meeting people can be hard and awkward, but networking is a trait you can learn. The more of it you do, the better you will become at it. I was a very shy person growing up, but I understood that if I was going to be successful in business I couldn't do it without customers and referrals. Socialize in settings where your potential customers are and join the associations they are members of. No one wants to go to a Monday night function, but you can bet that your successful competitors will be there. Believe it or not, you might also meet some great people who will become lifelong friends.

"The person who insists on seeing with perfect clearness before deciding never decides." - Henri Amiel

62. Remember People's Names

How many times have you been introduced to someone and immediately forgotten their name? Remembering names is an easy skill to learn. If you're unfamiliar with the process, it's called "word association," there are easy-to-read books on it. People love to hear their name, so use it in conversation as often as it is appropriate. This skill is necessary for your success because people like to associate with people, both personally and professionally, who they feel have a sincere interest in them. Using people's names in the electronic world we now live in, where the personal touch is fading away, is more important than ever. People are starving for attention and a simple thing like remembering their name goes a long way.

"The squeaky wheel doesn't always get the grease. Sometimes it gets replaced." - Vic Gold

63. Buy What You Need, Not What You Want

There is a big difference between a want and a need. The temptation to buy what you want can be extraordinary, but you must delay those purchases and let your money grow. You will get to a point in your life where you will be able to buy whatever you want because your net worth will be so high due to the discipline you had as a young person.

> *"The percentage of mistakes in quick decisions is no greater than in long, drawn-out vacillations, and decisiveness itself makes things go and creates confidence."* - Anne McCormick

64. Choose Your Spouse Wisely

There will be no bigger decision in your life than whom you choose to marry. Your spouse can greatly determine your happiness in life, which corresponds to your attitude at work. Be sure to marry a person who has great financial discipline and the same goal you have to be financially independent. A spouse that spends beyond his/her means will create great stress and agony in the marriage. Of course, there are many other qualities that you are looking for in a spouse—this book is purely focused on the financial traits.

"You don't give children everything they want without also giving them boredom." - Unknown

65. Don't Accept Money From Your Parents

After you have finally moved out of the house and declared your independence, don't ask your parents for money. You will never become truly independent if you know you can go back to Mom and Dad to bail you out. Most parents don't realize that they are hurting their children by always being there for them when things get tough financially. Keep yourself out of the financial cookie jar. If you do put yourself in a vulnerable position financially, look in the mirror and get yourself out of the situation you created.

> *"A child educated only at school is an uneducated child."* - George Santayana

66. Don't Become a Good Golfer

There is only one way to be good at golf: You must play a lot. From driveway to driveway, golfing is a six-hour commitment. Few people have this kind of time to waste more than a couple of times a year. I've heard every excuse about why people play golf, with the #1 response being "It's good for business." I believe that just as much business, if not more, can be accomplished over a one-hour lunch. Your customers will know if you play a lot of golf and you could lose some of their respect. They may prefer to deal with one of your competitors who is more accessible and serious about their business.

> *"Between saying and doing many a pair of shoes is worn out."* - Unknown

67. Stay Away From Activities That Drain Cash

There are many commitments you can make that will keep you from saving money. Expensive toys come along with monthly payments, not to mention insurance, taxes, upkeep, etc. Memberships are another way for your hard-earned cash to flow away from you. Every time you commit to a new monthly financial obligation you put one more hole in the dam—and I think you know what happens when there are too many holes. Be very careful about what bills you can handle coming into your mailbox every month.

"To escape criticism—do nothing, say nothing, be nothing." - Elbert Hubbard (American author)

68. Exercise Caution Before Signing Your Name

Make sure you read everything before you sign your name because in a court of law a judge is not going to have any sympathy for you when you say that you did not read the fine print. This pertains especially to contracts, because the stipulations can be extremely damaging to you financially if things don't go your way. It is a good idea to have an attorney read through a major document before you sign on the dotted line. A few hundred dollars in fees can be worth thousands or tens of thousands of dollars. If you are uncomfortable with the wording on something you are supposed to sign, have it changed or don't sign it.

"It is easier to become #1 than stay #1." - Unknown

69. Spend Cash

A credit card makes buying things way too easy and it gives people a false sense of financial well-being. When greenbacks are in your pocket, don't you notice that you are more apprehensive about spending them, as opposed to just pulling out a credit card? It's okay to keep a credit card with you in case of an emergency, or if you're renting a car, etc., but always spend cash when making a purchase. This is a great discipline and you will never have to worry about how you are going to pay your credit card bill.

> *"Most of us spend our lives as if we had another one in the bank."* - Ben Irwin

70. Large Savings is Not Dependent On Large Income

You do not have to make a large income to become financially independent. **Your financial independence depends on how much of your income you save and when you start saving.** (PLEASE RE-READ THIS TEN TIMES, AS IT IS THE MOST IMPORTANT SENTENCE IN THIS BOOK.) I feel I am beating the same drum throughout this book but it is totally up to you how you are going to work the equation. There are many people with modest incomes who are set for life because at a young age they decided to live way below their means. It truly is that simple—but you must have the discipline.

> *"There is nothing wrong with America that cannot be cured with what is right in America."*
> - William J. Clinton

71. Volunteer Your Time

It is important to be a good citizen. As a young person with limited financial resources, the one thing you can donate is your time. I liked coaching kids, but if that's too much of a commitment, there are several volunteer groups you can hook up with that will accept a few hours of your time each week. Not only does volunteering make you feel good, you will probably meet people who can help you grow your career. Just putting yourself out there and being active creates good things. People see you in a good light when they see you giving back to society. In reality, volunteering your time is self-serving!

"You cannot live a perfect day without doing something for someone who will never be able to repay you." - John Wooden

72. Walk Fast

You are probably wondering what a discussion about walking fast is doing in this book, but as I observe successful people, I notice that the majority of them move at a fast pace and are capable of doing multiple things at once. They are generally fidgety people and their brains move at the speed of light. When I was sixteen a mentor told me to walk fast because it would allow me to get more done. He also said that walking at a slow pace "just didn't look good." I have never forgotten his advice. I walk and move at a fast pace, which I think inspires the people working around me. If you move at a lethargic pace all day, you won't accomplish much and your hyper co-worker will be promoted right around you.

"Twenty years from now you will be more disappointed by the things you didn't do than by the ones you did do. So throw off the bowlines. Sail away from the safe harbor. Catch the trade winds in your sails. Explore. Dream. Discover." - Mark Twain

73. Nothing Replaces Face-to-Face Communication

Some people think they can make it through life depending on New Age technology. Let me make it clear: E-mails, voice mails, faxes, beepers, cell phones, etc., have their place in this fast-paced world we have created, but the best form of communication and relationship building will always be face to face. I delegate most of the electronic forms of communication so I am free to build relationships belly to belly most of my working hours.

> *"In order to succeed we must first believe we can."*
> - Unknown

74. Listen, Don't Talk

Make a conscious effort to stay quiet. You will learn much more by listening and the person you are with will like and respect you more. Let the other person be the smart one. You will come out the winner because people like to deal with people who make them feel good, which usually just involves good listening skills. While you are talking, the other person is thinking about what they are going to say anyway, so let them keep the floor.

> *"To improve your memory, lend people money."*
> - Unknown

75. Buy What You Need and Move Forward

Many people waste a lot of time shopping for the best deal. Let me help you: Retail stores know what their competitors' prices are and to stay in business they will be competitive. Buy what you need and move along. You should place a high value on your time and driving around all day to save $50 is a poor way to spend your precious life. Spend the time you save from shopping around working and building relationships. Not only will you be ahead monetarily, you'll have more time with family and friends, which is priceless.

> *"Man is still the most extraordinary computer of all."*
> - John F. Kennedy

76. Provide Exact Directions

I receive accurate directions about 30 percent of the time—and this drives me crazy. One of my professors at The Ohio State University taught me how to give directions when she gave me an F on a test that was simply to give directions from my campus dorm to downtown Toledo. I missed a lot of small details because I took things for granted. You must give directions like you are giving them to a first grader from London. Give people three times as many details as you think they need, and give them slowly. This may not seem like a big thing, but it shows your exactness and attention to detail, which are critically important traits.

"You're here for a short stay. Don't hurry, don't worry and be sure to smell the flowers along the way."
- Unknown

77. Send Handwritten Thank-You Notes

In this digital age, the handwritten thank-you note has become a thing of the past. Just think how you feel when you receive a handwritten envelope with a note to match inside. You will receive help from several people on your journey through life. Sending a personalized, handwritten thank-you will make such an impact that these people will want to help you more because they know how much you appreciate their assistance.

> *"People of great ability do not emerge, as a rule, from the happiest background. So far as my own observation goes, I would conclude that ability, although sometimes hereditary, is improved by an early measure of adversity and improved again by a later measure of success."* - Northcote Parkinson

78. Be Competitive

Most of us are competitive in differing degrees. The more competitive you are, the better your results. I am intensely competitive, but I do not show it outwardly to my customers. I want to win every deal and will work as long as it takes to figure out how I am going to achieve that. I can't stand losing, but I am not a sore loser. I learn from the deals that I don't get. A person with a passive personality will get run over and will not survive in the competitive landscape that exists in most businesses.

> *"If you see ten troubles coming down the road, you can be sure that nine will run into the ditch before they reach you."* - Calvin Coolidge

79. Use Personal Days Sparingly

Situations come up in life that force you to be away from work—but it should happen only once or twice a year. To show good faith to your boss, provide proof (if you can) that you absolutely had to take time off. Many people use up every personal day they feel the company owes them. These are the same people that will be replaced or laid-off first. If you milk the system, it will come back to haunt you. Don't think for a minute that your boss doesn't notice who is abusing the system. Your company must be able to count on you to be at work

---

"Ideas are a dime a dozen. People who put them into action are priceless." - Unknown

80. Eat Healthy Foods and Take Vitamins

I don't want to sound like your mother, but what you eat is important. If you want to live a long and healthy life you should have an established diet, including vitamins and supplements. Over time I've established a diet that has treated me well and has allowed me to never miss one day of work due to sickness, and I am forty. Avoid the lure of fast food on a daily basis. Eat plenty of vegetables, fruits, and grains.

"There is nothing permanent except change."
- Heraclitus

81. Don't Run Away From Your Debts

Declaring bankruptcy has become much too easy. It used to be a huge embarrassment, so it was a rarity. In how many advertisements do you see the phrase "bankruptcy—no problem"? Let me tell you, it is a problem. Losers declare bankruptcy. If you can't afford to pay back money you borrow—DON'T BORROW IT! If you ever find yourself in a position where you can't make your payments on time, sit down FACE TO FACE with the people you owe and work out an extended payment plan. Almost all financial institutions will work with sincere people who want to do the right thing. You never want to damage your credit rating because without friendly banks, you will have trouble moving ahead in this society.

"Not failure, but low aim, is a crime."
- James Russell

82. Take Calculated Financial Risks Along the Way

Whether you know it or not, you take several calculated risks every day. Your gut usually tells you whether you are making a good decision or not. As you accumulate money, you will have to decide where to invest. I suggest putting a little money in a lot of different places so if you make a bad decision (and you will) it will not wipe out your net worth. A financial advisor that you have researched and trust 100 percent can get you started. If you know successful people who will truly have your best interests in mind, ask them to steer you into some safe investments. As you accumulate more money, investment opportunities will come your way. There are more bad investments than good investments out there, so be careful.

"Let's talk sense to the American people. Let's tell them the truth, that there are no gains without pains." - Adlai E. Stevenson

83. Pre-Pay Your Bills in January

I may be the only person in the country that does this, but since I was twenty-one I've pre-paid all of my bills for the year in January. I am able to negotiate discounts for pre-payment on some of my upcoming obligations; although that is not the main reason I do it. I do it for the peace of mind of knowing my bills for the year are behind me. I can focus on building my savings and I am not distracted writing out ten or more checks every month plus doing all of the banking that goes along with that. This is one thing I do that doesn't make pure financial sense—but it makes me feel good and has allowed me to spend more time remaining focused on my financial goals.

"Whatever advice you give, be brief." - Horace

84. Set Your Sights on Forty

Ever since I was twenty, my goal was to be able to retire at age forty, if I wanted to. I was deathly afraid of having to work until I was sixty-five or seventy. Life is short and I wanted to enjoy it. I actually reached my goal a few years early by doing all of the things in this book. It is a great feeling to know I can do whatever I want and purchase anything I want. It is especially gratifying to donate money to worthwhile causes. Rest assured, I am just a normal guy who accomplished all of this—and you can, too!

"To achieve great things we must live as though we were never going to die." - Marquis de Vauvenarques

85. Buy the Best Quality Merchandise You Can Afford

You usually get what you pay for. If you buy junk, the product's life cycle is short and you'll have to buy again. If you purchase the best from the start, it will cost you less in the long run. I like to buy high-quality, name brand merchandise. People have told me that I am paying extra just for the name and they are wrong because the reason it is a brand name is because the product's quality has endured the test of time. Customers do not support brands that don't perform. In every product category, however, there are some obnoxiously priced brands that are geared to the elite in this country. Stay away from those.

"Think young. Aging is for wine." - Unknown

86. Embrace Change

There are thousands of stories about individuals and businesses that got left behind in the dust because they were not receptive to change. How many times have you heard people say, "I've been doing it like this for years"? You never want to recite that statement because closed-mindedness is now seen as a sign of stupidity. Whatever career path you choose, stay on the cutting edge—so you not only survive but also thrive.

> "In a progressive country, change is constant; change is inevitable." - Benjamin Disraeli

87. Simplify Everything

I take things that are complex and make them simple. This goes for almost everything I get involved with. Big, thick documents normally have only a page or two that are truly worth taking the time to understand; the rest is filler. In business you need to get to the point quickly. You will lose your audience during long presentations and in pages upon pages of documents. Some people think that complexity shows how smart they are, when in reality, short and simple shows true genius. People's attention spans have shortened over time since we are bombarded with so much information on a daily basis. It is your job to provide the bare, essential information that will deliver your intended message.

> *"The only thing we can do is play on the one string we have, and that is our attitude."* - Unknown

88. Be Accessible

Some people like to do their job from nine to five, go home, and not be bothered with work issues until the next day. There is another group who work all day long, but invite their customers and co-workers to call them after hours or on weekends if they are in a jam. Guess which group gets ahead in life? I've always been available to work Saturday and Sunday if needed, and all of my customers have my home phone number (which I put on my business card). I tell them to call me anytime. People would rarely call, but just knowing they could demonstrated my commitment to them and set me apart from my competition. Accessibility might lead to some inconvenience for you, but it is also an ingredient for success.

> *"No mistake or failure is as bad as to stop and not try again."* - John Wanamaker

89. Go Above and Beyond the Call of Duty

If you do only enough to get by at your job, everybody knows it, including the person responsible for promoting you. An employee that comes in early, stays late, works Saturdays, and does so with great enthusiasm will shoot to the top of an organization like a rocket. My philosophy is: "If you only want to just get by at work, you will just get by in life." I knew a salesman who wore a pin on his lapel that simply read "ABCD," which meant "above and beyond the call of duty." He was the top salesman in his 200 million dollar company. GO FOR IT!! STAND OUT!!

> *"It is my ambition to say in ten sentences what other men say in whole books."* - Friedrich Nietzsche

90. Technology is a Double-Edged Sword

I used to be anti-technology. I really fought it hard, but as soon as I started using it, I realized how much more productive and efficient I could be. The problem with technology, however, is that some people literally get buried in it and it becomes a negative factor. They forget to spend time with the people that they should have great relationships with, in order to advance their careers. How efficiently you use your time will determine your success. I am now a technology fan—but I realize that it will never replace me— just enhance what I can accomplish.

"They can because they think they can." - Virgil

91. Buy Supplemental Insurance When You Have a Family

Stuff happens! An unexpected accident that disables you for a while can be devastating, not only in lost income, but also medical bills that are not covered under your regular health insurance plan. I have a couple of friends who, thank goodness, had this insurance when devastating circumstances occurred in their lives. Three supplemental insurances everyone should have are disability, intensive care, and cancer insurance.

> "Children have never been very good at listening to their elders, but they have never failed to imitate them." -James Baldwin

92. Let's Talk About Retirement

The word "retirement" should be stricken from the dictionary. "Transformation" should be used in its place. I like the phrase "when will you be transforming" as opposed to "when will you be retiring?" It is a proven fact that some people who actually retire are dead within days. Maybe they should have tried transformation.

> *"And yet, despite this constant reminder, most of us go along using time aimlessly, failing to get out of it either enjoyment of life or the satisfaction of accomplishment."* - Unknown

93. Transform on Income-Generating Sources

At some point, you should be free from a daily work routine and be able to do what you want, as opposed to what you have to do. My goal is to have enough annual income from my investments (after taxes) to cover three times my living expenses when I make the transformation. I want a big buffer to compensate for inflation, a major financial disaster, or traumatic health events that could occur. Invest in things that generate monthly incomes, like rental properties, bank CDs, bonds, or personal loans that are secured by assets, etc.

> "If the creator had a purpose in equipping us with a neck, he surely meant us to stick it out."
> - Arthur Koestler

94. Don't Even Think About Social Security

I don't expect to see one dime of the hundreds of thousands of dollars I'll have contributed to Social Security over my lifetime. Social Security seems to be well on its way to insolvency as people are living longer and draining the fund. I believe the government will keep pushing back the age when benefits begin and/or deny benefits to people who the government feels do not need them. As my dad used to say; "You come in alone, you're on your own, and you go out alone." You must take total responsibility to build your nest egg and never think for a minute that Social Security will supplement your income. If it happens, great! But don't count on it.

"I have not yet begun to fight." - John Paul Jones

95. Generate a Personal Net Worth Statement Every Six Months

It is important to know exactly where you are financially. The only way to know if you are making progress building your net worth is to tally up your finances every six months. You need to set net worth goals and generating a personal net worth statement every six months will tell you if you are on track. As your net worth grows, you could have money in a lot of different places, and this list will remind you where it is. Also, if something unexpected happens to you, your family will have a current financial report. .

> *"If you're in a small boat, on a big lake, and a major storm rolls in, pray to God but row towards shore."*
> - Unknown

96. Diversify Your Portfolio

Some people have put all of their eggs (dollars) in one basket and lost everything. Many unimaginable things can go wrong with any single investment; you don't want to put yourself in a situation where one event can wipe out all of your savings. I probably have my money in twenty different places because I have worked so hard building my net worth that I never want to start all over again. If you diversify your portfolio, you will have some stellar investments along the way—and you will be tempted to funnel a lot of your money into that single investment. DON'T DO IT!! If a couple of investments go south, you won't be happy, but you also won't go broke. There's nothing wrong with making a little money in a lot of different places.

> *"Never pay attention to what critics say. Remember, a statue has never been set up in honor of a critic."*
> - Jean Sibelius

97. A Solid Strategy to Build Your Net Worth

You must commit to living way below your take-home pay. The balance of this money must go into savings and safe investments. If you continue to do this throughout your life, you will build a great net worth. Also, I use the income off of my investments to either pay down assets, like my house, or reinvest the money in other investments. This strategy keeps my net worth constantly growing. I want all of my money working for me at all times—and I never dip into money I've saved to pay for day-to-day living expenses. The strategy I have outlined is basic, but it does require great discipline. If you allow yourself to slip just once, and dip into your savings, you have allowed yourself to fail and you will do it again and again. Don't start.

> "When written in Chinese the word crisis is composed of two characters. One represents danger and the other represents opportunity." -John F. Kennedy

98. After You've Built a Great Net Worth, Donate

There is no correct amount to donate, but as my dad used to say, "Give until it feels good." While I was building my net worth I would donate $50 here or $100 there; but now that I can do more, I do. It is fun when you can make a big impact on a cause that you believe in. Don't wait until you die to be philanthropic. Give back while you are living.

> "A gossip is one who talks to you about others; a bore is one who talks to you about himself; and a brilliant conversationalist is one who talks to you about yourself." - Lisa Kirk

99. You May Have to Reinvent Yourself

After reading this book, you might feel you don't have what it takes to be financially independent. Maybe you don't practice many (any?) of the habits I've detailed. NO PROBLEM! DON'T GIVE UP. RE-INVENT YOURSELF! People do it all the time. Even if you can't master all of these habits, you certainly can obtain most of them. If you want to change and gain financial independence, you can. Don't let your mind hold you back. Look in the mirror and tell yourself that NOW is the time to change. The clock is ticking. You CAN do it!

"Best place to coach is an orphanage." - Bob Knight

100. The Future Has Never Been Brighter

usiness owners continually lament that, for the most part, the young people they hire are lazy, ambivalent, and unmotivated. This is a deadly combination but if I were you, I would see this as an opportunity. If you are enthusiastic, motivated, passionate, and driven you can literally write your own ticket to success! Your attitude, not your aptitude, will determine your altitude. If you adopt most of the traits in this book, you CAN'T MISS being a successful and vibrant member of society with a high net worth. And, you will be able to make the transformation from your full-time job several years before your peers. Start planning today!

One little six-year-old took home a note saying he need not come to school since he was "too stupid to learn." That boy was Thomas Edison.

FOOD FOR
THOUGHT

Happiness is a Journey, Not a Destination

Robert J. Hastings

Tucked away in our subconscious is an idyllic vision. We see ourselves on a long trip spanning the continent. Through the windows we drink in the passing scene of cars on nearby highways, of children waving at us from a crossing, of cattle grazing on a hillside, of smoke pouring from a power plant, of row upon row of corn and wheat, of mountains and valleys, of city skylines and village halls.

But uppermost in our minds is our destination. On a certain day at a certain hour we will pull into the station. Then wonderful dreams will come true, and the pieces of our lives will fit together like a jigsaw puzzle. How restlessly we pace the aisles, damning the loitering minutes—waiting, waiting—

"When I reach the station, that will be it," we tell ourselves. "When I'm eighteen." "When I buy a Mercedes!" "When I put the last child through college." "When I get that big promotion." "When I retire, I shall live happily ever after!"

Sooner or later we realize there is no station, no place to arrive at once and for all. The true joy of life is the trip. The station is only a dream that constantly outdistances us.

"Relish the moment" is a good motto, especially when coupled with Psalm 118:24. "This is the day the Lord hath made; we will rejoice and be glad in it."

So, stop pacing the aisles and counting the miles. Instead, climb more mountains, eat more ice cream, go barefoot more often, swim more rivers, watch more sunsets, and laugh more. Live life as you go along.

Success

Joseph Wade

If I wanted to become a tramp, I would seek information and advice from the most successful tramp I could find.

If I wanted to become a failure, I would seek advice from men who have never succeeded.

If I wanted to succeed in all things, I would look around me for those who are succeeding, and do as they have done.

A Story to Live By

Ann Wells (*Los Angeles Times*)

My brother-in-law opened the bottom drawer of my sister's bureau and lifted out a tissue-wrapped package. "This," he said, "is not a slip. This is lingerie." He discarded the tissue and handed me the beautiful garment. It was exquisite; silk, handmade and trimmed with a cobweb of lace. The price tag, with an astronomical figure on it, was still attached. "Jan bought this the first time we went to New York, at least eight or nine years ago. She never wore it. She was saving it for a special occasion. Well, I guess this is the occasion." He took the slip from me and put it on the bed with the other clothes we were taking to the mortician. His hands lingered on the soft material for a moment, then he slammed the drawer shut and turned to me. "Don't ever save anything for a special occasion. Every day you're alive is a special occasion."

I remembered those words through the funeral and the days that followed, when I helped him and my niece attend to all the sad chores that follow an unexpected death. I thought about them on the plane returning to California from the midwestern town where they lived. I thought about the things that she had done without realizing that they were special. I'm still thinking about his words, and they've changed my life. I'm reading more and dusting less. I'm sitting on the deck and admiring the view without fussing about the weeds in the garden. I'm spending more time with my family and friends and less time in committee meetings. Whenever possible, life should be a pattern of experience to savor, not endure. I'm trying to recognize these moments now and cherish them. I'm not "saving" anything. We use our good china and crystal for every special event-such as losing a pound, getting the sink unstopped, the first camellia blossom. I wear my good blazer to the market if I feel like it. My theory is if I look prosperous, I can shell out $28.49 for one small bag of groceries without wincing. I'm not saving my good perfume for special parties; clerks in hardware stores and tellers in banks have noses that function as well as my party-going friends. "Someday" and "one of these days" are losing their grip on my vocabulary. If it's worth seeing or hearing or doing, I want to see and hear and do it now.

I'm not sure what my sister would have done had she known that she wouldn't be here for the tomorrow we all take for granted. I think she would have called family members and a few close friends. She might have called a few former friends to apologize and mend fences for past squabbles. I like to think she would have gone out for a Chinese dinner, her favorite food. I'm guessing—I'll never know. It's those little things left undone that would make me angry if I knew that my hours were limited. Angry because I put off seeing good friends whom I was going to get in touch with-someday and being too busy to do the things I actually care about.

The Rest of Your Life
Begins Where You Are Now

Unknown

▲ George Foreman was forty-five years old when he recaptured the heavyweight boxing title and proved that youth and vigor are no match for wisdom and a solid right.

▲ Charles Goodyear was bankrupt and in jail when he finally perfected his process for vulcanizing rubber.

▲ Mary Kay Ash was close to fifty when she founded Mary Kay Cosmetics.

▲ Colonel Sanders received his first Social Security check on the day he decided to franchise his roadside fried chicken restaurant.

▲ Thomas Edison was still working vigorously in his seventies, directing research on torpedo mechanisms and anti-submarine devices for the U.S. Navy.

▲ Grandma Moses began her painting career at age seventy-eight and within one year became an overnight success.

George Brett on "How to Play the Game"

Personal Glimpses

No one ever played baseball harder than Kansas City Royals star George Brett. Once, when a reporter asked the three-time batting champ and future Hall-of-Famer what he wanted to do in his last at bat before retiring, he gave the following answer: "I want to hit a routine grounder to second and run all out to first base, then get thrown out by half a step. I want to leave an example to the young guys that that's how you play the game: all out."

Six Ways to Beat Procrastination

Unknown

Set specific goals. Don't make a vague promise such as, "I want to procrastinate less." Instead say, "I will spend two hours tomorrow straightening up my files."

Tackle the worst part first. Procrastinators are notorious for diving headfirst into simple tasks, then failing to get around to the most important work. Come tax time, don't spend hours gathering pencils and paper. Sit down now and start filling out forms.

Separate projects into small steps. Start on the piece of the project that is clearest in your mind, instead of diving into everything all at once.

Use small chunks of time. Have ten minutes when you're waiting for a meeting? Return a phone call or make notes for a letter you have to write.

Plan extra time. Procrastinators often underestimate how long it will take to complete a project.

Analyze, analyze. Take a notebook and spend a week recording all the things you're putting off. The second week, whenever you procrastinate, write down the excuses you tell yourself. Then ask yourself, "Is this excuse valid?" Finally, set up a system of rewards. For every week you meet deadlines at work, treat yourself to something you enjoy.

A New Day

Unknown

This is the beginning of a new day. I have been given this day to use as I will. I can waste it or use it for good. What I do today is important because I'm exchanging a day of my life for it. When tomorrow comes, this day will be gone forever, leaving in its place whatever I have traded for it. I pledge to myself that it shall be: Gain, Not Loss; Good, Not Evil; Success, Not Failure in order that I shall not regret living this day.

Failures . . . But Not Quite

Unknown

As a young man in Kansas City, he had a burning desire to draw. He went from newspaper to newspaper trying to sell his cartoons.

But each editor coldly and quickly suggested that he had no talent and implied that he might want to choose another line of work. But he persevered, determined to make his dream a reality. He wanted to draw and draw he would.

For several months, the rejections came. Finally, he was hired by a minister to draw pictures advertising church events. Working out of a small, mouse-infested shed owned by the church, he struggled to be creative. Ironically, this less-than-ideal working environment stimulated his most famous work. Fascinated by the mice running around his drawing board, he made the first sketch of Mickey Mouse. Later Walt Disney added Minnie Mouse, and began his long and illustrious career.

If I Had My Life to Live Over

Erma Bombeck

Iwould have invited friends over to dinner even if the carpet was stained and the sofa faded.

I would have taken the time to listen to my grandfather ramble about his youth.

I would have never insisted the car windows be rolled up on a summer day because my hair had just been teased and sprayed.

I would have sat on the lawn with my children and not worried about grass stains.

Instead of wishing away nine months of pregnancy, I'd have cherished every moment realizing that the wonderment growing inside me was the only chance in life to assist God in a miracle.

When my kids kissed me impetuously, I would never have said, "Later. Now go get washed up for dinner."

There would have been more "I love you's" and more "I'm sorry's" but mostly, given another shot at life, I would seize every minute . . . look at it and really see it . . . live it . . . and never look back.

MILLIONAIRE by 40
100 Secrets to Creating Wealth—Not Taught in School

is available at
www.Millionairebyforty.com